WHAT
IS
TRUTH

GARY MILLER

ISBN: 978-1-63813-128-1

Cover and text layout design: Kristi Yoder

Printed in the USA

Published by:

TGS International
P.O. Box 355
Berlin, Ohio 44610 USA
Phone: 330.893.4828
Fax: 330-893-4893
www.tgsinternational.com

WHAT
IS
TRUTH?

GARY MILLER

Introduction

I am a natural skeptic. Suspicious by nature, I have always lived with a fear of being deceived. I had good parents and listened to them (most of the time), yet I subconsciously questioned what they said. I tended to assume I wasn't getting the complete story. Going through life like this—suspiciously analyzing everything I hear—can be challenging.

Perhaps you can identify. Maybe you aren't sure who to listen to or what to believe—or whether absolute truth even exists. I understand! This little book is a hypothetical story that shares some of my own wrestlings with truth. Admittedly, hypothetical stories are created to make a point and are usually written to guide the reader to a predetermined outcome. So right from the start, I want to admit there are parts of this account that are presumptive. This narrative occurs on a university campus, yet it does not accurately portray normal life on the average college campus. Few professors on campuses today are as bald-faced or prescriptive about their beliefs. Yet the values and viewpoints articulated, I believe, embody what has become normal in our academic world. It is the air being breathed, even if seldom so overtly expressed.

My goal in writing is simple: I want to encourage the reader to investigate further, to not be discouraged by conflicting voices in our world. And to ultimately answer the question: "What is truth?"

1

"Six million years ago a female ape had two daughters. One became the grandmother of all chimpanzees. The other is your ancestor." Professor Ruth's deep voice paused. He peered over his glasses, which perpetually slid down his nose. "Remember that the next time someone insinuates you're someone special."

That does explain a few things, Steve thought wryly. He glanced down at his vibrating phone, then attempted to read the text without being noticed. Dr. Ruth, while friendly enough, had little patience for electronic distractions. Steve quickly scanned the message as the biology professor's voice droned on.

"If you could drop into eastern Africa as it was two million years ago, you would recognize much of what you observe. Much of it would be the same as today—mothers caring for children, young people chafing under the authority of elders, and tough young men trying to impress the girls."

Steve kept his eyes on the professor, but his mind was elsewhere. Steve's father, a natural entrepreneur, had founded an extremely successful software company. As a result, Steve had lived a life of privilege. Each year's income had exceeded the previous one, and Steve had grown up in luxury, enabling him to travel extensively. Most young men raised in similar circumstances would have been intoxicated with the status and wealth. But Steve had always been a little different.

On one hand, he was a normal young man who enjoyed his affluent lifestyle. At the same time, he had always felt a sense of loneliness and emptiness. Maybe this was partly due to his mother moving out when he was five years old. She had enjoyed her husband's wealth, but since he was seldom home, there was little relationship. Divorce seemed to be the obvious solution. Taking enough money to live comfortably, she had left. She called Steve occasionally, but he always sensed it was more out of obligation than love. Steve's father was almost never present either and tried to make up for it by surrounding Steve with an abundance of things. Steve's primary influence growing up had been a succession of nannies.

An only child, Steve had assumed his father's wealth would eventually be his. However, two years ago he had received a shock. The night before Steve left for college, his father sat down to have a talk. He informed Steve that he had selected the best university and spared no expense. "But now it is up to you," he said. His father had seen too many wealthy men give businesses to undeserving sons, only to watch the business eventually crash. "That isn't going to happen to my business," Steve's father told him. "If you dig in and excel, the business is waiting. But if you get sidetracked, plan on finding employment somewhere else!"

Steve knew his father would follow through with his threat. Yet he wasn't unduly alarmed. His grades were good, he enjoyed school, and he wasn't ready to settle down and make money yet anyway. He was much more concerned that the four years would pass without his deep inner questions being answered. It was here among the brightest minds on the planet that he hoped to get answers.

Steve had always been a researcher. His teachers said he was a natural scientist who wasn't afraid to disagree with the majority. Just because everyone else was proclaiming something to be fact wasn't enough for Steve. He wanted truth. That was why he enjoyed university life. There were so many opportunities to learn and to hear diverse opinions.

Suddenly a question from a student behind him pulled Steve from his reverie. "At one time, survival of the fittest was only a theory. But today we know Darwinian evolution is a fact. So why do people persist in embracing myths? Why do seemingly intelligent people, in spite of all the evidence, still believe there is some god who created everything?"

"Yeah," chimed in a student at the front. "I just had a guy give me a religious tract, trying to convince me the world isn't very old. I tried to be respectful, but the bottom line was, he had more confidence in his Bible than in the fossil record. He wasn't even interested in looking at the evidence!"

Groans and a few snickers followed. Steve rolled his eyes. He had run across a couple of those narrow-minded religious fellows as well. Most of them could easily talk about their creation story but were out to sea when confronted with facts.

Dr. Ruth nodded as he crossed the stage. His voice was sympathetic. "I understand your frustration. Remember, all through history humans have been slow to embrace truth. There was a time when men declared that the earth was the center of the universe. They believed the sun went around the earth. Even when confronted with scientific evidence, people refused to reconsider."

The professor stopped abruptly and faced the class. "And religion was often the obstacle that impeded such progress!" He smiled and let his words sink in. "But make no mistake. No matter what they say, science has the answers, and truth will eventually win!"

Class was dismissed. As Steve collected his biology books, he realized this final statement embodied what he liked about college. The pursuit of truth! That was why he loved science! He wanted solid, unshakable facts. Not some flimsy, outdated myths from years ago.

As a young boy, Steve had heard the story of Diogenes of ancient Greece carrying a lantern through the streets of Athens in search of one honest man. Steve had always identified with Diogenes' quest for honesty and had decided to pursue scientific truth until he had answers to his questions.

If Ruth were running for office, his campaign slogan would be "Ruth for Truth!" thought Steve with a smile. He exited the room and headed down the hall with his friend Vihaan.

2

It was ironic how quickly they had become fast friends. You couldn't have found two young men with more diverse backgrounds. Steve was raised in the midst of prosperity, while Vihaan grew up in a rural village in southern India, knowing nothing but poverty. Attending a prestigious university in America was like living in a different world. At times Vihaan felt guilty, knowing his family was still in a far different setting.

Vihaan's father worked hard when jobs were available, and his mother bought and sold in the local market. But they didn't own any land, and the intermittent income made life a constant struggle.

As soon as the children were old enough to work, Vihaan and his four siblings had been hired out to nearby farmers in the rice fields. It was difficult and backbreaking work, but the children were diligent workers. They knew the few rupees they earned were essential if the family was going to eat.

When Vihaan was ten years old, an international organization offered to pay for his schooling. For his family, this was like winning the lottery. Vihaan still remembered the excited look of hope in his parents' eyes. In spite of his youth, he was well aware that much rested on his shoulders. Young Vihaan was determined to make his parents proud. He would get a good education and eventually help his family rise out of poverty. He was under no illusion that this would be easy. Many youth in India were in sponsorship programs and competing to qualify for college. Yet Vihaan had succeeded, qualifying for a two-year degree and then obtaining a scholarship at this university. It had been hard work, but Vihaan was determined and blessed with a good mind.

Steve and Vihaan had become fast friends, admiring each other for different reasons. Steve saw Vihaan as extremely intelligent and admired his rise from humble beginnings. He loved to listen to Vihaan portray the difficulties and joys of growing up in a poor yet close-knit family. All Vihaan had ever known was a fight for survival. In contrast, Steve's own privileged life seemed superficial.

As the young men headed across the lawn toward their dorm, Vihaan provided an update from the humanities class he had just attended. "We looked at cultures where people spend their lives trying to make various gods happy. They live in fear of deities who could make their lives miserable if they are not appeased. Actually, some people in my country are very much like that. I couldn't help but think about my own family. I guess the best I can do is to be prosperous enough to help them. I must focus on being successful!"

Steve picked up a stick and flung it aside as they walked. "I wouldn't worry too much about that, Vihaan. With my connections to Dad's business, I think we can find a way to get you a well-paying job so you can help them!"

3

ihaan couldn't sleep that night. Steve's comment circled through his mind, giving him hope. Providing for his family in India was a burden that hung like a weight around his neck. If he could accomplish that goal, his father would be so proud of him! Since first meeting Steve, Vihaan had nursed this secret fantasy. With Steve's wealth and connections, surely he was the answer to his family's poverty. Vihaan couldn't help but be excited, but he would need to be careful. If he pushed Steve too hard, he might lose it all!

Seated on their favorite bench under a large oak tree the next afternoon, Steve and Vihaan watched several students playing Frisbee. "So, Vihaan, people say it's important to set long-term goals while you're young. What do you want out of life?"

Vihaan pondered the question carefully before responding. His life and Steve's were so different. Being too transparent might destroy his cherished hope. "I just want to work hard and do my best. What do you want out of life, Steve? It seems you already have everything!"

Steve looked out across the manicured lawn. "I grew up with lots of money, yet something was missing. I've always carried this inner sense that I'm missing some important pieces to life's puzzle. I came here searching for truth, hoping science will provide the answers."

A squirrel chattered overhead while the young men sat in silence. Suddenly Vihaan turned to Steve. "One thing I have never heard you talk about is religion. Festivals and Hindu rituals were a big part of my life in India. They were what my family talked about, planned around, and looked forward to. Hinduism was all I knew. But here I find all kinds of beliefs. There's a girl in my class who insists Islam is the answer. One guy wears a T-shirt saying stuff about

Jesus. Another girl meditates and talks about connecting with her higher power. Did you go to church when you were growing up?"

"No, neither of my parents were religious. My dad didn't have time for anything except business. Had I grown up in your setting, I would probably see religion differently. I respect your culture—and don't take this wrong—but I just don't have any interest."

"Maybe that's what's missing in your life, Steve. Perhaps an inner belief in something out there would provide some meaning." Vihaan squinted through the sunlight at his friend.

Steve paused. "It has always seemed to me that religious people have shut off their brains. I've read about Muhammad's archaic views and his abuse of women. And I don't see people who are deep into meditation spending less time with their psychologist than anyone else." Steve peered up into the tree. The squirrel's chattering had become increasingly loud and persistent. "I guess I would rather focus on things I can see than surmise about things I can't."

The squirrel continued scolding, and the two young men laughed at its antics. Then Steve continued, "One thing has perplexed me about this religion thing. On campus we have a Buddhist meditation park, and we have designated yoga rooms. There is toleration for religions, and you can believe pretty much whatever you want. But my professors consistently attack Christianity. Why can't they tolerate that one?"

Vihaan pulled out his water bottle and took a drink before responding. "Probably because of the impact it has had on American history and culture. Or maybe because Christianity is the largest." His tone was dismissive. "I need to get back and attack my homework."

Walking toward their dorm, Steve broke the silence. "I have to admit this pursuit after truth isn't as easy as I thought it would be. Even our professors don't agree. Ruth says science has—or will soon discover—the answer to every question. He sees truth as absolute, and science as eventually possessing the solution to every dilemma. On the other hand, Dr. Hoover in Anthropology vehemently disagrees!"

Vihaan laughed. "From what I've heard, those two have had a friendly feud for years."

"I know. The Science and Humanities departments have long been engaged in an ideological battle. Both sides have interesting and compelling arguments. It makes my pursuit of truth more difficult. It'll be interesting to hear what Professor Hoover has to say tomorrow. His lecture is titled 'Questions Science Is Incapable of Answering.' "

"Interesting!" Vihaan replied. "I almost wish I had taken that class!"

4

"Maybe you came to college searching for truth." Dr. Hoover's voice captivated the class. He was affectionately known as Smooth Hoove, due to his ability to fascinate and persuade. He was also known for his friendliness; the students could depend on Hoover's help when they were in a pinch. "Perhaps you hoped to find ironclad answers—irrefutable facts—something solid to provide reference for life." Dr. Hoover paused and smiled. "While this was more common in the past, my guess is there are still a few of you on a quest for the meaning of life, hoping to find absolute truth."

Steve sat, eyes glued to the professor. *I am definitely*

one of those few, he thought ruefully. *At least Dr. Hoover understands what we're looking for!*

"If that is your goal, you've come to the right place. But before proceeding, you need to confront a popular delusion: the idea that life's toughest questions can be answered in a scientific laboratory. You will hear that from educated people—maybe right here on this campus. But think carefully before embracing it."

Silence covered the room.

The professor smiled before continuing. "But don't worry; I won't leave you without a solution. In the next class I will share my personal beliefs and how I have found rest with this issue. But first, let's start by proving that science has not provided answers for many of life's pressing questions."

The video projector sprang to life, throwing the title "Questions Science Is Incapable of Answering" onto the screen.

"Science is studying structures and behaviors in our natural world through observation and experimentation," the professor explained. "Its primary concern is with observable and repeatable events in our physical universe. Consequently, despite what you may hear from other professors, science is limited."

A hand shot up near the front. "I don't believe anything exists beyond our physical universe, so why is science incapable of answering my questions? Since I only believe in observable facts, why would I bother with anything besides science?"

"Ah, so you have decided to only believe what you can observe. How many of you agree this is a rational approach to life?"

Most hands went up, but Steve hesitated. Something about the way the professor asked the question gave him pause. Dr. Hoover's reputation for well-thought-out arguments was legendary, and Steve didn't want to start the day looking like a fool.

"Let's start with a simple question: How many of you believe Julius Caesar lived?" Every hand went up. "I'm assuming you can prove his existence scientifically. Can you present observable and repeatable facts that clearly substantiate your belief?"

Uncertainty filled the air as the question settled in.

"Unfortunately, science provides answers to only a small range of questions. If you want to know whether Julius Caesar lived, science provides no conclusive evidence. We can find observable writings about him, sculptures of what he supposedly looked like, and plays about his death. But after you've assembled all those clues, you still have to decide if you will believe or disbelieve the evidence. You can't see or test Julius Caesar's existence. All this supposed evidence could have been created just a few hundred years ago in an effort to fool us."

Several hands were in the air, but Dr. Hoover ignored them. "Understand, there are enough clues out there that only a fool would deny Julius Caesar existed. Yet I would argue you can't prove his existence scientifically."

Hands went back down, and the professor let the thought sink in. "The claim that science is all-encompassing is a philosophically indefensible position. Let's look at another question."

Dr. Hoover advanced the PowerPoint, projecting the next question: "Why is murder wrong?"

"I'm assuming all of us agree that homicide is unacceptable. But why? Of course, we know that societies that fail to protect their citizens don't survive. But can you prove scientifically that murder is wrong? Of course not. It's a moral issue. Science is incapable of assisting us in making moral decisions."

The next question flashed onto the screen: "Is there

a god?"

"Can you prove scientifically that a god does or does not exist? Is that observable? If not, how can you substantiate your conclusion on this topic? Ladies and gentlemen, this list goes on and on. Anthropology can take us back and show us how belief in a deity affected cultures, but this isn't within the realm of science.

"Believe me, there are many questions science is incapable of answering. What about the awareness of our own existence, or of human consciousness? Can a scientist observe it under a microscope? Can he weigh it on a scale? What about emotions? Can you watch a feeling?"

Dr. Hoover continued flashing questions onto the screen, calmly driving his point home, before turning off the projector.

"I have asked nuclear physicists what energy is, and they can't tell me. They can tell me what energy does, but they can't define what it is. Amazing! That should be easy for a scientist.

"And what about the big question all of us ponder from time to time: What happens after death? Personally, I don't believe anything happens, but I didn't reach that conclusion because the scientific community presented evidence. I have simply chosen to believe that death is the end."

The professor's arguments brought even more questions to Steve's mind. A student behind him verbalized one of them. "So, if science isn't equipped to answer these questions, where do we go? Some of these issues need to be resolved."

The professor smiled and nodded. "We will address that in our next class. Please understand, science has its place. Wonderful things have been discovered via the microscope and telescope. But science *is* limited. Consider the number of galaxies said to be out there. Back in my college days, confident professors told us there were millions of them. We believed what we were told. In those days a million was an incomprehensible number—and whenever scientists run into something inconceivable, they like to smother it with incomprehensible numbers."

Dr. Hoover smiled, then continued in his patient and persuasive manner. "Over the years, the supposed number of galaxies has kept changing. Now they are saying there may be trillions of them. What was presented as truth when I was in college isn't considered truth today, and what you are hearing now will be outdated in a few years. Friends, this is because we forget the role of science. The role of science is to focus on things that are observable or repeatable. In other words, it is to be sitting squarely on facts. So how many galaxies are there?"

The only sound was of students shifting in chairs.

"The truth is that astronomers don't know. They can't see all the galaxies. Frankly, this isn't science at all. It's guessing. For all we know, there are an infinite number of galaxies out there! Astronomers don't want you to consider that, because they like to portray their latest guess as truth.

"When I was in college, we were taught to trust science. We were told that the answer to global peace was increased scientific discovery and development. Admittedly, we have seen progress. But science has also brought pollution, global warming, and the atomic bomb. Instead of delivering world peace, humans have found more efficient ways to destroy each other. So much for science being the answer!"

Glancing at the clock, the professor saw it was time for dismissal. But Hoover was clearly enjoying himself. Lowering his voice, he continued, "For that matter, I don't classify evolution as science. It is neither observable nor repeatable. So frankly, it is just a theory. Show me proof of one species evolving into a more advanced species. Just one! Show me a scientist who has observed something being created from nothing. Show me a big bang without inputs. Furthermore, show me order and intricate detail resulting from a massive explosion! Until you can show me those things, let's call evolution what it is—it is choosing to believe in the unseen."

There was silence for a moment. "Evolution actually has all the characteristics of a religion. Personally, I believe evolution may be true. Not because of scientific proof, but because it's the only good option for origins. Besides, I like the idea that we have evolved. I like to think we have advanced to the top of the evolutionary pile due to self-focus and choices based on our own well-being." With a shrug and a smile, he concluded, "But at least I am honest enough to call it what it is! It's just a theory I happen to like. Class dismissed!"

5

Back under their favorite tree, Steve and Vihaan began their typical afternoon rehash. Other than the squirrel loudly protesting above, this setting was an oasis from the campus rat race. "Ol' Smooth Hoove was at it again," began Steve, "and he was persuasive. His goal was to prove that science can't answer all our questions. What happened in Philosophy?"

"It was a lecture on absolute truth versus relative truth. The professor said every culture creates its own set of moral judgments that become a reference point. He said nothing is inherently or universally right or wrong, but over time humanity has learned which moral laws are most effective. That is why we see such moral continuity across the world."

"Interesting. Any good discussion?"

Vihaan laughed. "Most of us like to think that absolute truth exists and that science will eventually provide answers. But one guy said it isn't possible to be absolutely certain about anything. Somebody asked if he was absolutely certain about that. Of course everyone hooted, and the class sort of fell apart at that point."

Steve threw a stick up into the tree in an attempt to quiet the squirrel. "It's confusing. Ruth, in Biology, says absolute truth is out there, and science is gradually revealing it. But Hoover, in Anthropology, insists that there are many questions science is incapable of answering. He's like your philosophy teacher. He sees truth as relative, and thinks each of us needs to find the truth that works for us. It's no wonder the student body is perplexed."

Steve stood up, trying to see where Mr. Squirrel had taken refuge. The first stick had sent him scurrying up the tree, and his scolding had intensified. Raising his voice, Steve continued, "Frankly, college has disappointed me. I had assumed that with all these intellectuals, I would find irrefutable answers to my questions. Instead, while the professors are pleasant, polished, and polite to each other, they don't seem to care about coming together on solid answers to difficult questions. They remind me of this squirrel. Their primary goal seems to be defending their own intellectual turf."

Looking up at the deeply offended squirrel, Vihaan laughed. "There definitely is a resemblance! Like the squirrel, they have strong opinions but seem incapable of articulating solutions."

Steve sent another stick higher into the tree. The squirrel retreated further and finally quieted down. "But Vihaan, here's what bothers me. I'm not looking for material to prove others wrong. I just want to build my own life on reality. Dr. Hoover says that in his youth he trusted science, and it let him down. I don't want to look back fifty years from now and realize that my life has been based on a false premise. I'm tired of theories. I want foundational truth that is demonstrable and works in real life."

"Typical math and science guy!"

"That's why I came here, Vihaan. I want to see something that works!"

"How will you know when you find it? What if everything is just random, and there *is* no ultimate cause or reason?"

Steve watched as a robin landed a few yards away and began looking for a worm. "I have trouble believing that. There is an underlying harmony in our ecosystem. Whether you're looking at astronomy, botany, or biology, nature hums along like a well-oiled, finely tuned machine. With the exception of humans, who keep messing things up and appear to be headed in the wrong direction, every species seems to have a specific role it is supposed to fill—and it is filling it. Is it logical to say there isn't a reason or purpose for all this?"

"Oh, great. Next you'll be telling me there is some wonderful, altruistic designer who created all this. If there is a god, and he is good, I have some big questions for him! Like, why has my country experienced so much poverty and suffering? That speaks of randomness to me."

The robin found its meal and pulled the unwilling worm from its home. The young men laughed over its accomplishment before Vihaan continued, "What makes you think our culture isn't heading in the right direction? We are making tremendous strides in communication, transportation, medicine, and any other field you can think of. Why would you wonder if we are on the right path, or suspect our professors don't have the answers? Is it just because they don't all agree?"

Steve sighed. "No, it isn't that they can't agree. I can deal with that. Everyone is entitled to his own opinion."

He took a drink from his water bottle. "What bothers me the most is the sense that these highly educated professors, in spite of their well-crafted arguments, are still missing something vitally important. You'd assume a person who has pursued education and scientific reality all his life would have greater fulfillment. You'd think he'd be able to interact harmoniously with other humans. But I haven't observed this. They're all nice enough, but they are continually vying for more power. Just like everyone else, they have difficulty keeping their marriages intact and seem to need frequent trips to their psychiatrists to stay sane and functioning. I don't want to be fifty years old and dependent on counselors and pills!"

Vihaan laughed. "I understand! But at least things work here in America. In India we can't even afford psychiatrists! Or pills!"

Steve stuffed his books into his bag. "Many things are better here, but I'm not sure people are more fulfilled. You didn't grow up with money, but your relationship with your parents is much better than mine. I barely know my father, and my mother rarely calls. It's becoming clear to me that wealth is over-rated. It can't provide the things that matter most."

Walking across the lawn, Steve continued, "The lives of many Americans seem pretty dysfunctional. It makes me wonder if anyone out there has answers. Seriously, Vihaan, do you know any professors who are living lives that exemplify who you want to be in thirty years?"

Vihaan didn't answer. As the two walked on, Steve continued to verbalize his inner ponderings. He didn't notice, but Vihaan had stopped listening. Vihaan had come to America for one purpose—financial success for himself and his family. Steve's friendship and likely involvement in his father's business had seemed to be his best hope for fulfill-ing that goal. Now Steve was denigrating American prosperity, even hinting that people in countries like India might have more fulfilling lives.

Vihaan couldn't help but feel nervous. Anxious thoughts circled through his mind. *What if Steve decides to abandon his father's business? What would happen to my dreams and my family's future?*

6

"One of the theories you will hear certain people pontificating on is the idea that absolute truth does not exist. This argument has been all the rage the past few years. The thought is that immutable truth does not exist, and the idea should be abandoned."

Flicking on the projector, Professor Ruth explained further, "We are going to be looking at theoretical biology. It is essential that you understand the importance of irrefutable facts. It is foundational!"

Removing his glasses and whirling them as he paced, Ruth dove into his subject. "First, let's define terms. When we talk about absolute truth, we are talking about inflexible reality. This is the idea that truth is fixed, invariable, and unalterable. One of the strong opponents of this concept was the humanist John Dewey. Dewey emphatically stated, 'There is no god and there is no soul. Hence, there is no need for the props of traditional religion. With dogma and creed excluded, then immutable truth is dead and buried. There is no room for fixed and natural law or permanent moral absolutes.' "

Professor Ruth paused and chewed on the earpiece of his glasses before continuing in his deep voice. "How many of you agree with Dewey's statement?"

A few immediately raised their hands, but others obviously had some trepidation about committing. A part of Steve wanted to agree, but he suspected they were being led into a trap. "Do you mean the part about there being no god?" he asked. "Or the statement about immutable truth?"

The instructor chuckled. "I am assuming most of you are rational thinkers and have concluded that there is no god. I know there are still a few stragglers, but for the most part society has moved on. Just the other day I had a conversation with one of the maintenance men who still believes there is a god. But my question refers to the second part. Does absolute truth exist?"

He dropped his glasses on the podium and looked out over the class. "I see about half of you agree with Dewey, so let's start with you there in the back row. Why do you believe Dewey was correct?"

The young man had obviously given this topic a lot of thought. "No one's opinion is any more valid than anyone else's, so everyone has the right to create his own set of values. The instant you decide there is a hierarchy of truth, someone's truth becomes of lesser value. The only way to avoid this messy quagmire is to decide there is no standard, and each person has the right to develop his own."

Remembering Vihaan's class, Steve considered asking the student if he was absolutely sure about his position. But before anyone could raise his hand, the professor responded.

"Okay, so you are absolutely sure that absolute truth doesn't exist? For the moment, let's assume you are right. There is no standard for truth, and each person has the right to determine right and wrong for himself. How would a society like that function? Would you all be okay if I abused a child? Or if I murdered my neighbor because he parked his car in my driveway? If it's okay with me and my truth, does that mean it's fine?" Professor Ruth put his glasses back on and patiently looked over the class. "After all, isn't this the basis of evolution? Isn't it is the evolutionary right of each species to conquer those who are less fit? Why shouldn't the stronger take advantage of the weaker?"

This started a lengthy debate. It was obvious the topic was a hot one. Most felt a society or culture must determine its own rule of law, yet they didn't like the idea of a stronger country bombing a weaker one when their rules of law didn't coincide. Steve wished Vihaan could be here to listen. Eventually Professor Ruth felt he had made his point. Most agreed that for world peace to prevail, some kind of common reference point was needed.

Glancing at the clock, the professor brought the argument to a close. "We need to wrap this up, but obviously this dialogue could go on for a long time. In spite of the position of some of my friends in other departments, relative truth is a dead-end street. It won't work in world politics, and it will not work in this class. In fact, why argue anything if there is no standard of truth? How would you know who is right? Once you decide there is no absolute right and wrong, you have no basis to be angry at any injustice. If it's not wrong, why get upset when the weak are violated or when someone cuts in front of you in line? Despite what you may hear in other classes, truth must be absolute. Science cannot operate without it. The fact that people keep arguing about it proves that absolute truth does exist!"

Silence blanketed the room as the students considered the professor's logic. Gathering his papers, he offered his final thoughts. "I'm not saying you should allow religious extremists to set the rules. Neither am I saying that science has arrived at a complete understanding of absolute truth in all spheres. But given enough time, I believe science will reveal a complete view of reality.

"For those of you still entertaining the erroneous belief that each person's viewpoint is as valid as anyone else's, understand this: there is a time coming when your performance in this class will be evaluated." Professor Ruth paused and dramatically lowered his voice for effect. "Rest assured that at that point my opinion will be of greater value than yours!"

The students laughed, but as Steve left he soberly reflected on Professor Ruth's comments. The professor's logic was simple: science depends on absolutes. If absolute truth doesn't exist, further study is useless.

As Steve told Vihaan later, his mind was beginning to feel like a ping-pong ball. Each class provided logical arguments. When Ruth promoted truth, it made sense—even though his arguments directly contradicted Dr. Hoover's!

7

teve didn't expect his next class to decrease his mental tension. As he walked into Smooth Hoove's anthropology class for Part 2 of "Questions Science Is Incapable of Answering," he knew he was in for it again.

"In our last class we surveyed several important questions that science is not capable of answering. I mentioned historical questions, such as whether Julius Caesar actually was the Roman military genius we think he was—or if he even existed. We also looked at the inability of science to observe human consciousness or emotion. My goal was not to undermine the beauty of science. Rather, it was to demonstrate its limitations."

Picking up Professor Ruth's biology textbook from the podium, Dr. Hoover opened to a section on the human body. He began to read. " 'Ninety-six percent of the human body is made up of just four elements: oxygen, carbon, hydrogen, and nitrogen. The remaining four percent is a sparse sampling of the periodic table of elements.' " Closing the book slowly, he looked up at the class. "How many of you believe one of our renowned scientists could take these basic elements, utilize modern technology, and create a human body?"

Silence.

"Why not? Didn't the science book just give the components of a human body? Are you telling me that with all our modern discoveries, all our brain power, and all the high-tech scientific equipment available today, we still can't accomplish what supposedly happened by itself in some primordial swamp?" Dr. Hoover smiled as he walked back to the podium. "Oh, I know what they will say. When facing the improbability and irrationality of their theories, they love to throw in a few more billion years. As I stated earlier, I suspect they are simply guessing!"

There was a sudden shifting in the front, and a science major raised her hand. "That doesn't seem like a fair assessment. If you are going to disparage evolution, you should at least come up with an alternative."

"Fair enough. But remember, I didn't say evolution didn't occur." Leaning against the podium, Dr. Hoover's voice softened. "Let me begin by sharing my personal beliefs and where truth can be found. I will start with my personal beliefs. You recall that I started out majoring in science but became disillusioned when I didn't get adequate answers to difficult questions. For example, spontaneous generation is too simplistic an explanation for the beginning of the complex life we observe. It is statistically impossible for the incredible intricacy we see around us to have come from nothing. But neither do I know where it came from. So I have embraced an agnostic position. When pushed by either evolutionists or proponents of intelligent design, I just say I don't know, and that gets them off my back."

Starting his customary pacing across the room, Dr. Hoover continued, "The problem with deciding what is true on some of these issues, or if absolute truth even exists, is this: it opens the door for a group of people to declare that they possess this truth. This has happened all through history, in every culture. And as soon as this occurs, someone feels guilty because he is disobeying the standard. That is a miserable place to be. I have chosen to avoid this by giving each person the liberty to possess his own truth.

"Of course, for thousands of years religious people have declared that absolute truth exists. Some of those people are still out there. If I was willing to listen, they would gladly explain their truth to me." Dr. Hoover groaned and rolled his eyes. "I feel sorry for those religious fanatics. But I just remind myself they possess their truth and I have mine."

Lying in bed that night, Steve tried to process the arguments from the day's lectures. Professor Ruth had made a good case for absolute truth. *If there is no standard and every person's opinion is equal, why grade papers? Why even go to school?*

But Professor Hoover had refuted that with some good points. *If absolute truth exists, then not everyone can be right. It requires some to be wrong.* As Steve considered that position, his thoughts traveled further. *But if everyone has a right to his own opinion and survival of the strongest is at work, how can anyone say a man like Hitler was doing wrong? He was simply the strongest man in Germany at the time. He was just exerting his evolutionary right to dominate and impose his beliefs on others.*

Glancing at the clock, Steve realized he'd been wrestling with these questions for over two hours. *If none of this matters, why can't I just go to sleep?* Yet he knew why he struggled. His life was before him, and he longed to pour his energy into something that was true and worth living for. Steve rolled over, trying to find a comfortable position. *Maybe I am looking in the wrong places. I need to be open to every possibility, regardless of how unlikely or weird.*

Steve had no idea how weird things were going to get!

8

"Hi! It sounds like you have a problem." Steve was very glad to see the smiling maintenance man at the door. He had used every towel in the bathroom to try to minimize the damage until a repairman could get there.

"Come on in. I heard something dripping under the sink and looked to see what was happening. Then, when I tried to mess with it, it started spraying water everywhere. That's when I called." Still holding a soaked towel, Steve led the way to the bathroom.

"No problem. That's why we're here." The man quickly reached down, turned a handle, and the flow of water ceased.

Steve was amazed. He felt a little foolish for the trouble he had caused. "Thanks. I guess it pays to know what those knobs are for down there!"

The man laughed. After a quick investigation, he stood up. "I need to get a couple parts. By the way, my name is Mike Jackson."

"I'm Steve. Thanks for coming so quickly."

Mike soon returned and repaired the plumbing. With the problem taken care of, Steve headed for class. He had enjoyed the brief interaction and was glad the leak was fixed. He had no idea his path would cross Mike's again—or how deeply this man would challenge his life.

It happened at a university event. Each spring the chairman of the science department invited students to an evening presentation entitled *Facing the Facts*. The program was much anticipated by the students. Posters around the school shared tantalizing bits of information to help build excitement as the event approached.

The purpose of the program was to share scientific developments such as new fossil findings, genetic discoveries, or other evidence specifically related to the evolutionary development of life on earth. In the past, there had been debates when the evidence presented was controversial. Consequently, most students wanted to be present and adjusted their schedules accordingly.

On the evening of the event, Steve was doing homework when he suddenly realized the presentation was about to start. Racing across the campus, he slipped into the auditorium just as the lights were dimming. Realizing that the seats were full, he joined other latecomers along the back wall.

The first speaker shared information from a recent study on the evolution of the human genome. He was clearly excited. As Steve tried to listen, he suddenly realized the older man next to him wasn't a student. In fact, it was the plumber. In his maintenance uniform! Steve was perplexed. Maintenance men were supposed to fix air conditioners and stop leaks under students' sinks. They were supposed to do whatever else uneducated people do to keep their family fed—not listen to scientific presentations on the human genome.

During the intermission, Steve decided to indulge his curiosity. As the lights went on he turned to the maintenance man, glancing at the name on the nametag to be sure he remembered correctly. "Hi, Mike. Are you enjoying the lecture?"

"Yes, there's a lot to think about. How about that sink, Steve? Everything working well?"

Steve was a little stunned. Out of all the students on campus, Mike had remembered his name.

"Yes, you obviously knew what you were doing."

"Great! So, Steve, why did you decide to attend this event tonight?"

Steve was momentarily taken aback. His eyebrows flew up in surprise. This was the very question he had been prepared to ask Mike! Something about Mike's candid demeanor made him want to be straightforward in return.

"I love facts, which is probably why I like science. My life goal is to pursue truth. That is one of the reasons I'm attending college."

"So how is your search going? Would you say you're finding satisfactory answers to your questions?"

Again Steve paused. This man had an uncanny ability to put his finger on the problem, just as he'd done when diagnosing the plumbing problem in Steve's room. Suspicious he was being ridiculed, Steve looked into Mike's face. He was met with brown eyes that spoke of genuine concern, not mockery.

Looking down, Steve responded thoughtfully, "I'm trying to sift through many diverse opinions, so I've made few conclusions. But I'm not in a hurry. I'm trying to thoroughly consider each perspective."

"Have you identified what it is you're looking for?"

Now here was a puzzler. Steve hesitated. What *was* he looking for? He wanted to say "absolute truth," but he wasn't certain that even existed. Before he could formulate a respectable response, Mike continued, "Don't rush to answer. You'll find many individuals here who are searching for something, but when asked, they're not sure what it is. I encourage you to begin by defining what you are searching for." Mike's smile was sincere. "After all, if you don't know what you're looking for, how will you know when you find it?"

Mike was interrupted by his buzzing phone. "Looks like I have to go. They have a problem in the kitchen and I'm on call. Nice to meet you, Steve. Let's chat again sometime."

As the evening progressed, Steve's mind kept returning to that brief conversation. It wasn't just the questions Mike asked, but also the genuine concern he showed. There was something about Mike that was . . . well . . . different! The man was obviously uneducated, yet he asked such good questions. They were simple, basic questions. That last one kept going through his mind: *"What are you looking for?"*

Steve knew he wasn't alone. He had friends who were also searching for reality. He knew they weren't as confident as they liked to pretend. The late-night dorm discussions revealed that the weekend partying was, to a large degree, an attempt to mask reality. Many of his fellow students were living a charade, appearing to be poised and assertive when in reality they were seeking something—but not sure what. Maintenance Man Mike's question was spot on: "Have you identified what you're looking for?"

9

"Vihaan, it was crazy! It was like the man had been listening to our conversations! Here he was, a maintenance man with a screwdriver in his back pocket, asking me profound questions." Steve looked puzzled and a little ashamed of himself. "I guess I assumed people like that don't have intelligent thoughts."

Vihaan leaned back against the park bench and considered. "I wish I could have been there! This is weird. Did you learn anything more about him?"

"That's the strange thing. I wanted to learn why he was attending an event like *Facing the Facts*. But it turned out he interrogated me!" Steve's brow creased.

"It wasn't just what he said. There was something different about him."

"Different? Wouldn't that be true of any guy who lives in America, the land of opportunity, yet chooses to work on dirty pipes?"

Steve watched as a jet left a trail of white across the sky. "No, it was something else. I need to do what he said—figure out what I'm searching for. Most of us, and even our professors, are dealing with two recurring questions: Does absolute truth exist? And if it does, where is it found? I want something that works. I don't want to be fifty years old, grouchy, and dependent on pills and counselors to stay sane."

"But Steve, as long as you have financial resources, anything is possible. How can you go wrong?"

"No, Vihaan, wealth alone is not the answer. My father gave me sufficient evidence to debunk that theory. I'm pretty sure that maintenance man with grease under his fingernails is getting more joy out of life than my dad ever did."

Vihaan threw up his hands mockingly. "Oh, great! Now the answer to life's questions is to join the maintenance department!" They both laughed. Secretly, however, Vihaan was concerned. He was well acquainted with the problems of poverty, and to hear Steve devaluing the pursuit of wealth was disturbing.

"Steve, maybe Hoover is right and you are taking the pursuit of truth too seriously. If truth is within us, why not follow your own desires. Just do what feels right to you."

Steve scuffed the toe of his tennis shoe against the ground. "On the one hand, that argument sounds attractive. But I'm not willing to give up so easily. If we all make up our own truth, why does anything matter? No, I'm not ready to throw in the towel. I'm going to keep digging. In fact, tomorrow I'm going to chase down that maintenance man. He left a screwdriver in my room. Returning it will give me a chance to ask him some questions!"

· ·

The maintenance building was an unimpressive concrete block building located just behind the football stadium. Steve had never even known it existed and had to get directions to find it. Walking in, he found himself in a lobby at the end of a hallway leading to several offices. It was still early morning and no one was in sight. Steve paused, unsure where to go.

Suddenly he became aware of a discussion in one of the rooms. An agitated young woman was speaking. "How can you know for sure that God exists? This world is full of pain and suffering. Just last week there was another earthquake in Southeast Asia. Hundreds of little children were killed in a mudslide. If there's a god up there, why doesn't he do something? Do you know what I mean?"

The words echoed down the concrete hallway. Then a voice Steve instantly recognized as Mike Jackson's quietly responded, "I understand what you are saying."

"Sometimes I wonder if life is worth living!" the troubled girl continued. "I have been to counselors repeatedly. And when I talk to my professors, they just recommend a different one. I know you are a Christian, but I will tell you up front—I don't have much use for religion! My parents were religious hypocrites. They went to church, but our home was a mess. Eventually they divorced. I came here looking for answers. And I'm not finding much clarity!"

The young woman was almost shouting now, and Steve looked around uncomfortably. The respectful thing to do would be to sneak out of the building before anyone saw him. Yet the investigator in him realized this discussion might be helpful in his own pursuit of truth. His curious side won out. Taking a chair along the wall, he grabbed a magazine and pretended to read.

How much do we really know about God anyway? he wondered. *We have a few ancient scraps of text, written thousands of years ago by people who claimed to have heard or seen something. The whole thing sounds pretty sketchy! I hear that the writings contradict each other. And we're supposed to believe them?*

For a moment there was silence. The young woman was clearly struggling emotionally. Steve waited to hear a response. He hadn't known Mike was a Christian, and he wondered how he would react to this attack on his religion. Mike's response wasn't what Steve expected.

"Teresa, I know you are going through a difficult time. I am sorry. Your boyfriend has left you, you don't feel loved by your mom, and you're not sure where your dad is. That's enough to shake anyone. I wish there was some way I could eliminate the pain you are going through."

Steve could hear weeping, then everything was quiet. After a time, a chair scraped the floor and a tremulous voice said, "Thanks, Mike. It helped to stop by and unload. I need to get to class. I'd better go."

"Teresa, before you go, here is my wife's phone number. If you need someone to talk to, she would be glad to meet with you." The girl didn't seem to notice Steve as she passed on the way out.

Steve sat for a moment, analyzing what he had just heard. *This guy seems nice, but he ignored her questions! She brought up some pertinent issues, but he sidestepped them!*

Steve walked over to the door and knocked on the jamb. "Hey, Mike! I'm just returning a screwdriver. But, um . . . do you have time for a couple questions?"

Mike looked up from his cluttered desk and smiled. "Hi, Steve. Sure! Come on in."

10

Steve and Vihaan found a quiet table along the wall in the dining hall. Before they had set their trays down, Vihaan erupted with a volley of questions. Steve had arrived late to his first class after spending over an hour in Mike Jackson's office. Since Steve was normally very punctual, Vihaan knew something unusual had occurred.

"So what happened after the girl left?"

"Well, my original goal was to see what makes the man tick. But after I heard him avoiding her questions, I decided to attack his faith until he responded. So I dove right in! I told him I had overheard the conversation and didn't think he was fair. The girl had asked legitimate questions and he had avoided them. I told him I don't believe in blind faith. I want solid evidence before I believe something. I asked him if he has proof for his religious beliefs. And if so, I'd like to hear it."

"Let me guess. He asked you another question and avoided that one."

Steve set his untouched sandwich back down. "He didn't say anything at first. It was almost like he hadn't heard me. But then he asked how I knew I was born on my birthday.

"What does that have to do with it?"

"That's what I told him. In fact, it irritated me! But I told him I have a birth certificate. He asked how I know it's not forged. He explained that faith is believing something we haven't seen. So all of us have faith, whether we're talking about the date of our birth, historical events that happened before we were born, or scientific facts we haven't personally researched. He said he believes light travels at 186,000 miles per second, though he hasn't done the research himself. He has faith that the men who did the research knew what they were doing, and he has chosen to believe it."

Vihaan frowned. "Well, of course, whether it's science or religion, some faith is required. But surely he would acknowledge that most scientific facts are easier to prove than religious tenets."

"I didn't ask that directly, but he insinuated that many people are not considering all the facts."

Steve glanced at his watch. "Class starts in ten minutes. But here's the interesting part, Vihaan. Mike's office walls are covered with books. He's obviously an avid reader! Not your typical maintenance man, is he? He doesn't seem to be afraid of anything. But neither is he embarrassed to say when he doesn't know or isn't sure about something."

Vihaan laughed. "So he neatly destroyed your maintenance man stereotype. Where do you go from here?"

"He offered to continue our discussion, so we're meeting again later this week." Steve got up to return his tray, then paused. "There's something I forgot to mention. He had a mug on his desk with a strange quote." Pulling a scrap of paper from his backpack, Steve read, " 'Christianity has not been tried and found wanting. It has been found difficult; and left untried.'

"I wonder what that means. What kind of truth does he have that hasn't been tried? He sounds like a religious nut peddling a new twist on an old myth." Steve stuffed the paper back into his pack. "But I'd like to ask him about it."

11

"So, Mike, you claim to be a Christian. I have two questions. First, why would you believe in the God of the Bible? And second, why would a Christian be interested in an event like *Facing the Facts?* I don't believe in a creator, so of course I'm interested in seeing new evidence explaining how the universe began. But why would *you* go? I mean, the whole thing is devoted to presenting evidence that disproves the need for a creator!"

School was over for the day. Steve had spotted Mike working in a utility room and had stopped to talk. Mike put down his wrench and perched himself on a stepladder.

"Good questions, Steve. I was there because I love to learn. I don't always agree with everything that's said, but I usually hear something that makes me think about things from a different angle."

"I'm sorry if my questions sounded offensive. I'm just trying to be honest. I've tried presenting facts to religious students here on campus, and they don't want to listen. I've concluded they like faith but not facts. They evidently grew up in homes where they were taught one way to think and have never recovered!"

"I'm sorry that has been your experience, Steve. I was raised in a home like you described. My parents always went to church on Sunday. From my childhood, that's all I knew. Looking back, I wouldn't say my parents were devout believers, but we went to church and did what churchgoers do. But in eighth grade I began to have doubts. I have always loved facts, and I began to notice that the people in our church interpreted evidence in a way that was consistent with their belief, while ignoring the obvious."

Steve leaned forward. Mike was obviously an unusual religious fanatic. "I think I know what you mean, but can you give me an example, Mike?"

"Sure. Let's imagine an older lady from church stepped off a curb and was narrowly missed by a bus. She would stand up the next Sunday and tell how God had saved her from danger, and everyone would agree that God had spared her life. However, if the bus had hit her but she wasn't killed, everyone would say God had saved her life. And if she was killed, everyone would say God had taken her to heaven, which was better anyway. No matter what the circumstances, they always found a way to make God look good. As a young man this bothered me. Do you follow?"

"Absolutely. I have always wondered why religious people constantly spin their stories to make their god look good. If there were an all-powerful God, he shouldn't need defending!"

"That was my thought. It seemed no matter what happened, they had predetermined that God was good and felt obligated to prove it. There were no exceptions. There were certain questions no one asked. Like why a loving and all-powerful God allowed that bus to come along in the first place. When I asked a question like that, people seemed uncomfortable. Does that make sense?"

"Absolutely. What did you do?"

"I concluded that Christians are more interested in protecting their faith than in analyzing facts and facing reality."

. . . .

Early the next morning, Steve and Vihaan met at the track to exercise. Walking briskly around the athletic field, Steve conveyed yesterday's findings. As he relayed Mike's childhood experience and disillusionment with Christianity, Vihaan was intrigued. "So even as a child he could see his parents' unwillingness to look at reality."

"Yes, and it impressed me. The man was brutally honest about their hypocrisy and lack of interest in pursuing truth."

"But, Steve, if he is objectively pursuing truth, why is he a Christian? For me, Hinduism is different. It's more of a cultural thing, a way to understand life. But believing that someone two thousand years ago was killed and came back to life? Come on! How can you claim to love facts and truth, yet believe this stuff? It makes no sense!"

"Exactly! We spent some time talking about the problems he saw with religion while growing up, but then another worker came in and interrupted our discussion. As I was leaving he said he would like to continue our discussion. I really want to hear the rest of his story. He invited me to his home this weekend. Want to come along?"

12

The Jackson family lived on a three-acre property a few miles from town. As Steve and Vihaan pulled in their gravel driveway on Saturday afternoon, they weren't sure what to expect. Mike introduced the young men to his wife Myra and their three children. The children then returned to the pond where they had been playing, and Mike invited the young men to take patio chairs on the porch. As Myra served iced tea, Mike picked up his story where he had left off.

"I told you a little about my disillusionment with religion when I was a teenager. What I really wanted my whole life was to go to college. I wanted to learn!

I didn't want to sit around listening to unseen and unproven philosophies. I wanted scientific facts! But financially that wasn't possible. My father's business was struggling, and all of us children needed to help out. But I read every scientific journal and textbook I could get my hands on."

One of the small children soon returned and crawled into Mike's lap as he talked. Steve found his gaze shifting to the child. Something about the happy son, trusting and content on his father's lap, touched Steve's heart.

"Eventually, through a government grant and a part-time job in the maintenance department, I was able to enroll. I left home and started attending right here at this university. I came with high hopes. I was finally liberated from all that religious drivel and was free to pursue truth!"

Mike looked at Myra and they smiled.

"I came here assuming the answers could be found in education and scientific facts. I wanted solid evidence for everything. But something strange happened during my second year in college. I began to realize my college professors were sounding a lot like the church-goers I had come to despise. You see, anytime they came across evidence that disagreed with their theories, they weren't interested!"

Vihaan shifted nervously. "I'm sorry to interrupt, but it's one thing to entertain different philosophies or to debate opposing scientific theories. It's quite another to declare that a man rose from the dead! That borders on insanity!"

The porch was silent for a few moments. Vihaan, ashamed of his emotional outburst, blurted out, "Sorry, I didn't mean to come on so strong."

Myra quickly reassured him. "Don't worry, Vihaan. Mike understands your feelings well." She chuckled. "I remember him making similar statements not so many years ago."

"She's right, Vihaan," Mike said with a smile. "I made some pretty strong statements about Christianity. But let me continue. One of my first struggles was with origins. There are only three possible ways to explain the existence of the universe. Either the universe created itself, or it has always existed, or some external force created it. Those are the only options I have ever heard discussed. In college, only two of these theories were open for discussion. Any idea, regardless how implausible, was acceptable as long as it supported either the universe creating itself or having always existed. But if anyone dared to suggest the possibility of an outside force being involved, the idea was immediately scorned. You understand what I'm saying?"

Steve nodded. His eyes were on the child who had now fallen asleep in Mike's arms.

"Now, we know no human saw the formation of the universe. And since science by definition is constrained to the observable, this question is actually outside its bounds. In other words, since we can't observe first-hand how it came into being, all we can do is make assumptions from observable facts. Consequently, what we believe about the origin of the universe is a matter of belief."

"You're saying that since we can't observe or reproduce this phenomenon," Steve interjected, "the issue of origins is in the realm of faith, not science."

"Right. But what bothered me the most as a student was how opposed my professors were to even discussing the possibility of a higher power, or intelligent design. I started feeling the same frustration I felt as a young man when the churchgoers weren't interested in science. Both were forcing the facts to fit their dogma."

Steve glanced at Vihaan. "I understand. But this still

doesn't explain why you became a Christian."

Mike smiled. "Okay, I'll try to make the story brief. As I continued through school, I kept assuming I would find answers to my questions."

"What questions were bothering you?"

"There were three primary issues that troubled me. First, as I mentioned, was the issue of origins. Before you can talk about the *survival* of a species, you must first have the *arrival* of that species. I saw the scientific community on a pursuit after an explanation—any explanation other than religion—to answer the question of beginnings. I listened to everything from the extremely improbable to the absolutely absurd. Something about that desperate quest troubled me.

"The second issue was complexity. The further I got into molecular biology, the more obvious it became that there had to be a designer. Chance, regardless of how many million years you throw in, does not increase information. That's a huge problem for proponents of evolution.

"Third was the issue of purpose. Something deep within told me I am not a cosmic accident. There is a purpose for my life, and I wanted to know what that was."

A shout echoed from the pond. Mike looked over to where the children were playing before continuing. "Further, as I observed the lives of our instructors, I saw brilliant intellect but couldn't find one person I wanted to emulate. There were relationship conflicts at work and marriage problems at home. Everyone seemed very self-focused. Despite their relentless pursuit of self-fulfillment, I didn't see anyone who was fulfilled."

Steve leaned forward. The similarity of their searches was uncanny. "So what did you do then?"

"Myra and I were married by this time. She had come from an atheistic home, so her experience was completely opposite. We decided to set aside all of our prejudices and rethink everything. We were convinced that absolute truth existed somewhere. We didn't want to build our lives on something we would later regret."

Steve and Vihaan sat for a moment in silence. Finally Vihaan spoke in an incredulous voice. "And you ended up believing in Jesus Christ?"

Seeing the expressions on their faces, Mike laughed heartily. "Before you decide I am deluded and mentally incompetent, let me tell you how we came to that belief." He smiled broadly and chuckled. "I can see I'd better talk fast."

13

Myra returned with a fresh pitcher of iced tea. The little chap on Mike's lap woke and headed back to join his siblings. The youngsters appeared to be dismantling a bike close to the pond. Tools were scattered in the grass. "I lose more tools than I wear out," Mike muttered as he surveyed the scene before continuing his story.

"There were very few religious professors on campus when I came. I soon noticed that if an instructor had an ethical stance connected to his religion, there seemed to be an assumption that he was not being objective. Conversely, if he had no ethical stance, there was an automatic assumption that his research was objective. That strong bias raised my curiosity. If God doesn't exist, why all the fuss? I don't see this same angst over the Easter bunny."

Vihaan broke in. "Isn't that because the underlying tenets of Christianity have been investigated and found inadequate?"

"That's what I would have initially argued," Mike responded. "But the investigator in me wanted to hear all sides. I was looking for irrefutable evidence— solid proof I could observe with my own eyes. And I found it in an unusual way. I was still in school, and we had been married for a couple years. We were looking forward to our first child, so we began to discuss child raising and what we wanted in a family. As we looked around, it was discouraging. We didn't see anyone, let alone families, we wanted to model our home after."

Vihaan nodded. "I can understand that! Most American homes seem almost dysfunctional."

"We were living in town," Mike continued, "and a family moved in next door. I don't know how to describe them other than saying they were just different. We got to know them well. Their children fussed like any other children, but there was an underlying peace in their home that we had never seen before. The husband obviously loved his wife. He couldn't hide it! They honestly enjoyed being together! They weren't always watching television to be entertained. In fact, they didn't even own a television! They just liked being together! So we started asking questions. They weren't pushy, but they kept pointing to their faith in Jesus Christ."

Myra chimed in. "In the evenings they would sit on their back porch and sing together. We were so enthralled that we often turned off our television and went outside to listen!"

Mike laughed. "Now understand, I had strong objections to Christianity. Just seeing this family wasn't enough to dispel my doubts. Remember, my parents also said they believed in Jesus, and their home was very unhappy. But we were seeing enough to give us pause. As time went on, I realized I needed to investigate further."

"Maybe they just had personalities that blended well," Steve suggested, a little defensive. "I'm sure there are atheists who have nice families that get along well too."

Vihaan nodded, "We have many families in India

who enjoy spending time together. It's much different than in America!"

"Exactly. Myra and I talked about that. In fact, we knew another family in town who got along well. The parents were agnostics. So our neighbor family's behavior alone wasn't sufficient evidence for Christianity. But it did grab our attention. I realized the home and church I grew up in might not have represented the real thing. As we became better acquainted, we learned that this family wasn't alone. There were other families out there just like them. I was still not convinced. But it was enough evidence to cause me to rethink my position."

Silence reigned for a moment before Steve pressed on. "Okay, so how did you conclude that the message of Christianity was worth embracing?"

An argument suddenly erupted between two of the children down by the pond. Myra headed toward the disagreement. Mike continued his narrative, with one eye on the fracas. "I knew that the entire Christian faith was based on the supposed resurrection of its founder. If you eliminate the resurrection of Jesus Christ, you eliminate Christianity. So I decided to eliminate that first."

"But how can you go back and prove one way or another if a man rose from the dead?" Steve protested. "It's been two thousand years! How could you be sure? I mean, how could you be sure enough that you would base your life on it?"

"Good question! That was my dilemma. I began employing the research skills I was learning in college. I started by examining the historical Biblical record. Can the Bible itself be trusted? Is it a reliable historical document? I ignored what the Bible says about itself and went after historic facts. Did secular history agree with what is found in the Bible?"

Mike paused, reflecting. "All through college I had heard that there were many errors in the translation of Scripture. That today's Bible is not trustworthy."

Steve's eyebrows went up. "What did you find?"

14

Myra returned with two sniffling children in tow, both declaring their innocence. Evidently only one adjustable wrench could be found, and both boys had declared sole ownership. The sharp disagreement had turned physical, so Mike took the boys aside and spent a few minutes talking to them. After settling them on porch chairs, he returned to the conversation.

"Steve, I approached the topic of Biblical authenticity with severe doubts. I had given up on religion in general, so I was highly skeptical. I determined to research it myself. If someone else had done it, it would have accomplished little. Let me say this: If you are serious about finding truth, it is there. There is no shortage of verifiable facts if you are willing to research with an open mind."

"So you're saying I need to do my own research," Steve interrupted. "Fair enough. Go on."

"After researching the historical reliability of the Biblical text, I went on to investigate the lives of the men who were eyewitnesses—the men who would have known the truth about the resurrection."

Mike paused with a serious look on his face. "Steve, cover-ups happen all the time. After President Nixon's Watergate failure, his close associates were involved in a cover-up. They were eyewitnesses. They knew what had occurred. All of them initially lied about what had happened. They maintained this false position for about three weeks. But when it became obvious they were going to jail if they didn't change their story, they told the truth. They were not willing to sit in jail for a lie."

"How does that relate to the resurrection?"

"It's quite simple. Jesus' close followers were eyewitnesses of the resurrection and wrote down what they saw. These men were eventually tortured because of their statements, but not one of them recanted, though they could have saved their lives by doing so. Men don't die for something they know isn't true. History is clear: These men knew Jesus rose from the dead."

Vihaan had heard this argument before. "But what about Muslim suicide bombers? Are you saying their religion is true because they're willing to die for it?"

"Good question, Vihaan. But remember, radical followers of Muhammad weren't eyewitnesses of Muhammad. They never saw Muhammad, so their belief is not based on what they saw. They can't prove that what they've been taught is correct. Jesus' disciples were different. They would have known if there was a cover-up. If the resurrection was a conspiracy, they would have recanted. Men don't go through torture for something they know is a lie."

There was silence for a moment before Myra spoke up. "We spent a lot of time researching historical data. We had to! We wanted a solid foundation in our search for truth. But there was something else we couldn't deny. That was the difference we observed in the lives and families of those who followed Jesus. After several years of research, we had to admit that all the evidence pointed in one direction. And Mike was too much of a researcher to ignore the facts."

15

A little overwhelmed with Mike and Myra's story, Steve and Vihaan stood up to leave, thanking Myra for the iced tea. They had much to think about. Mike walked them out to their car, along with his sons who were happy to be released from their chairs. "Thanks for coming! I really enjoyed our time together! Any other questions before you leave?"

Steve and Vihaan looked at each other. They were both wondering the same thing, but weren't sure if they should ask. Finally Vihaan took the plunge. "Yeah, Mike, but I'm not sure how to ask it. It has to do with your occupation." He looked uncomfortable.

Mike laughed and leaned against their car. "You

don't need to feel bad, Vihaan. What you're wondering is why I went to a prestigious college but ended up being a lowly maintenance man. Is that it?"

Embarrassed, Vihaan shrugged. "Not saying there's anything wrong with it, but it is unusual."

"I was glad you understood plumbing when my bathroom was flooding," Steve interjected, trying to make everyone comfortable.

"No problem, guys. Let me tell you what happened. I came to college to learn, but I was also determined to make it good financially. I didn't want to be poor like my dad. Myra came from a different background. Her parents were wealthy. She grew up with plenty."

"I wouldn't say it quite like that, Mike." Myra had walked up in time to hear Mike's assessment. "We had plenty of money, yes. But very little of what actually matters in life."

Vihaan frowned. "What do you mean, what actually matters? Some Americans think poverty sounds kind of romantic. Having experienced it, I don't think you know what you're talking about!"

There was an awkward moment before Myra responded. "Good point, Vihaan. It is important to have enough to provide for your family. But you can have lots of money, yet be extremely poor. Some people equate financial wealth with success. That is a huge mistake. Sorry, Mike, I think I derailed your conversation."

"That's fine. And I'll make it brief. When I found truth in Jesus, it changed everything. I lost my passion for wealth and possessions. The bottom line is this: I really enjoy my job, and it provides a good income. As a side benefit, it allows me to keep up on scientific progress. Even though I don't agree with everything, I'll probably always be an incurable learner."

Myra laughed as she put her arm around Mike. "That's an understatement! If there was an award for irrepressible curiosity, Mike would win! But there's another reason Mike loves his job—he likes hanging out with students like you!"

Driving back to the campus, neither Steve nor Vihaan spoke for a few minutes. The conversation had obviously impacted Steve, and Vihaan was alarmed at the possible ramifications. *What if Steve falls for this Christian voluntary poverty stuff?*

Finally Steve broke the silence. "Pretty weird stuff,

hey Vihaan? What do you think?"

"Just another religious nut. All Mike's arguments haven't changed my opinion. It's as impossible to believe as ever—that a couple thousand years ago in the Roman Empire an unmarried teenager had a son who died, and that this somehow affects my life and provides answers to today's questions."

"Yeah, it's pretty wild. I will have to say though, there's something fascinating about Mike's family. Even the look in their eyes is compelling!"

16

The next day during lunch in the dining hall, Steve revived the discussion. "I keep going back to the question Mike asked me when we first met to talk: 'What are you searching for?' I sat in class this morning listening to Ol' Smooth Hoove describe, as only he can, the beauty of relativism, and how it's possible for two facts to contradict each other and yet both be true. Even though Hoover is a persuasive guy who's fun to listen to, his arguments seem increasingly implausible."

Steve took a bite of sandwich before continuing. "But just knowing there must be absolute truth doesn't tell me what is true! Professor Ruth says science will eventually reveal truth, but Mike believes he's already found it. You can't deny that their family seems happy and content. And happiness and contentment are rare commodities these days!"

"Maybe you're overthinking it, Steve. Maybe the harmony we observed in Mike's family isn't due to their religion. Maybe it's simply a result of having disciplined lives and a common cause. After all, my family in India likes to hang out together as well."

"Maybe. But whether they're deluded or not, there is something attractive there. Did you see how that little boy curled up in Mike's lap? There was something so beautiful and compelling about a child totally trusting his father, and the father enjoying a close relationship with his child."

Steve pulled a scrap of paper from his pocket. "Remember this saying from Mike's mug? 'Christianity has not been tried and found wanting. It has been found difficult; and left untried.' Now that I know more about Mike's ideology, that statement makes me curious. How can he say Christianity is untried? Christianity has more flavors than an ice cream shop! I'm also intrigued by his comments about the authenticity of the Bible and the resurrection."

Later in the day Vihaan had an experience he decided to keep to himself. He had walked into the Student Center where several students were studying.

"Hey, Vihaan, I heard you went to the maintenance guy's house to learn about Christianity. Did he get you converted?" Several students laughed as Vihaan set down his books and rolled his eyes.

"It was Steve's idea. And no, he didn't persuade me."

"Mike is an interesting guy," one of the girls chimed in. "I was there one time. I really like his wife! She just loves children. She originally majored in elementary education. After they became Christians, she decided staying at home and adopting a few neglected children would have more impact."

"Those aren't their own kids?" Vihaan was startled.

"No, and I was pretty impressed. Watching those children play—and realizing how different their lives could be—was moving. Mike and Myra believe in taking a grassroots approach to changing the world. There are others in their church doing the same thing."

Oh boy, Vihaan thought. *This is serious. If Steve*

hears about this, he'll be even more attracted to their beliefs!

"Their church is different than most," added another student. "Last year one of the foreign students had a big medical bill. She didn't have any way to pay it. And would you believe it—when she went to work out some kind of payment plan, they told her the bill was almost completely covered! All the hospital would tell her was that several people had been sending money anonymously. A little sleuth work revealed that this had happened before, and Mike's church was involved."

Listening to these stories caused Vihaan to become alarmed. He knew this would be incredibly attractive to Steve. What if he embraced Mike and Myra's beliefs?

17

"Good questions, Steve, and I'll do my best to address them." It was early morning. After ensuring Mike's office door was closed, Steve had dived into more of the issues that bothered him about religious faith. The night before, Vihaan had reacted angrily when Steve mentioned Mike's name, so he hadn't told Vihaan he was meeting with Mike.

"As you know, Steve, I can't prove to you that Christianity is true—not anymore than I can prove that Thomas Jefferson was an American president. There is a mountain of evidence, but neither of us saw Jefferson, so we must decide if we are going to believe the historical record or not."

"But how did you determine that the Bible is historically accurate? How can we be sure the writers weren't just biased and trying to foil us with a hoax? Almost everyone agrees that the Bible is full of errors, and if I told people I believed it was a historically accurate document, I would get laughed out of the classroom!"

Mike smiled. "Believe me, I understand the ridicule you would receive. But before you pitch the Bible, I would ask you to do something. Ignore the campus skeptics and do your own research. Very few of those talking the loudest have spent time exploring its historical authenticity. There has actually never been a book more thoroughly scrutinized, and there's no shortage of historical evidence.

"When I finally had the courage to analyze the Bible with an open mind, it wasn't what I expected. It wasn't about blind people accepting what someone told them. Some of the writers themselves were eyewitnesses to the resurrection of Jesus. Some other writers expressed the same deep suspicions about God that I had. There was Job, a man who had lost everything, sitting on a pile of ashes and wondering what was going on. This wasn't a brainwashed non-thinker. Even in the midst of misery, he was pondering the same questions we contemplate today. 'If a man die, shall he live again?'[1] he asked. And, 'What is the Almighty, that we should serve him?'[2] You may not like what the Bible says, but anyone who is willing to do his own objective research cannot easily dismiss it."

"But Mike, the Bible could have been written by some religious fanatic a couple hundred years ago. You weren't there. Maybe it isn't as old as you think."

"Even if we set the Bible aside, we still have volumes of other writings written by early believers during the first few hundred years after Jesus. Some of these authors personally knew the first followers of Jesus. These are historical documents: letters written to other leaders, encouragement to new believers, even letters to the Roman emperor who was in power at the time.[3] If the Bible suddenly disappeared, there are so many quotes within these writings that we could reconstruct almost the entire New Testament. There is no shortage of early supporting documentation. The idea that the Bible was concocted centuries later is ludicrous."

"Okay, I hear you. I know I'm being difficult, but

let's just say I decide to reject all that as well."

Spinning his chair, Mike pulled a stapled set of papers from the shelf behind him and handed it to Steve. "Here is a list of historical accounts from my research that reference Jesus or His followers in the first few centuries after Jesus. The authors of some of these, like the Jewish historian Josephus,[4] were born a few years after the death of Jesus. So they were able to observe his immediate followers firsthand. Others, like Tacitus, a Roman historian, wrote about Jesus and his followers a little later. Remember, men like Tacitus were opposed to Christianity. We wouldn't expect them to agree with the Christian message. If Jesus never existed and the entire thing was a hoax, surely they would have exposed the myth. But they didn't."

Mike paused a moment to let that sink in. "For centuries, no one tried to say Jesus wasn't an actual man who walked on earth and died on a cross at a specific location. Only in recent history, with the current atheistic push, has this ridiculous notion been promulgated. We live in a confusing time, Steve. With so many people trying to promote their own view of history, a man has to really love, want, and pursue truth to find it!"

For a moment Steve sat in thought. He had to admit he had never researched any of this himself. In fact, he couldn't remember talking to anyone who had. Everyone just "knew" the Bible was a man-made book. They just "knew" Jesus was someone like a lucky charm for uneducated people to believe in, instead of facing reality.

He decided to probe deeper. "Earlier you talked about your parents' lack of logic. You used the illustration of a woman getting hit by a bus. You said Christians tend to arrange facts into their preconceived beliefs. Why would you align yourself with a group of people notorious for using poor logic?"

Mike laughed and leaned back in his chair. "But it's not just religious people who do this, Steve. Most people tend to discard any fact that doesn't agree with their position. Remember, that's why I became disenchanted with the science department. The important question is whether you are willing to objectively search for truth. Very few are."

18

Steve glanced at his phone and realized he'd be late for class again if he didn't hurry. But as he rose, he spotted the coffee mug. That puzzling phrase had been circling through his mind for days.

"Mike, your coffee mug says, 'Christianity has not been tried and found wanting. It has been found difficult; and left untried.' What is that supposed to mean? How can anyone say it hasn't been tried?"

Mike picked up the mug and regarded it fondly. "There's some personal history here. The gist of the quote isn't original with me. G.K. Chesterton, an English writer, authored a book in the early 1900s entitled *What's Wrong with the World*. I read that book during my search for truth. In that book, he writes, 'The Christian ideal has not been tried and found wanting. It has been found difficult; and left untried.'[5] I kept thinking about that statement. What did he mean? As I continued my research, his message became clear."

"Which was . . . ?"

"As I grew up in a Christian home and attended a Christian church, everyone around me said they were following Jesus. They parroted all the right verses, yet something was missing. It was like they were children doing charades, acting out something they didn't actually possess. Even as a boy, I could see people claiming to follow Jesus even though their lives carried little resemblance to His teachings."

"So why join them?"

"Charades are interesting. There is usually an authentic reality behind them. In other words, when children act like a firefighter putting out a fire, they are pretending. But they are acting out something that is real. Just because they are play-acting doesn't mean there aren't real fires and real firemen. I decided to set aside the religious charade I had been surrounded with and go look for the reality behind it."

"What did you find?"

Mike laughed. "I'm not going to do your research for you, Steve. But I'll say this: If you investigate the Bible and the writings of the early church in the first few hundred years after Christ, you will discover that Jesus is more than you imagined. And Christianity is delightfully different than you suspected."

There was an uncomfortable silence as Steve tried to get his mind around this statement.

"But Mike, there are literally thousands of Christian denominations out there. I'm assuming they disagree with each other or they would be worshiping together. How would I sort through all of them? How did you?" Again Steve checked the time and realized he needed to go—now. Instead, he added another question: "And assuming I wanted to research Christianity, where would I start?"

"I would start by investigating who Jesus was—and is. When Jesus was here, he made some incredible claims. Many people approach those claims illogically. They say Jesus was just a good man. But his words don't give us that option. Jesus claimed to be the truth,[6] and He claimed divinity![7] C.S. Lewis, a professor at Cambridge, used to say that any man who went around claiming he was God would never be considered a good moral teacher. 'You must make your choice,' Lewis said. 'Either this man was, and is, the Son of God, or else a madman or something worse.'[8] Lewis was right. There is no middle ground! That is where all of us must start. You need to determine who Jesus is!"

. . . .

Steve lay awake for a long time that night. He had repeatedly declared that he wanted truth. But what would happen if he took Mike's advice and researched the authenticity of the Bible and the resurrection? What if he discovered the evidence was too strong to disregard?

The thought shook him. He realized the cost could be extremely high. His future, his status with his friends, even his friendship with Vihaan would be jeopardized.

On the other hand, could he live with himself if he refused to do the research?

Epilogue

We live in a confusing time. With the increase of technology, we're awash in information, with what seems like an opposing opinion on every corner. Emails, text messages, phone calls, social media, podcasts, newsfeeds, and more threaten to engulf us. The amount of information can be overwhelming, and many feel justified in concluding that absolute, universal truth doesn't exist. They decide that truth is relative—that people must find their own "truth." Underlying this concept is the idea that we are all different and the truth that works for one might not work for another.

But I find humans to be amazingly alike, possessing

very similar basic desires. Wherever you go around the globe, regardless of the culture, there is a general longing for a world where love, joy, and peace prevail. There is a general craving for caring communities where everyone belongs—a place where loneliness is banished and individuals treat others like they want to be treated. This inner desire is universal. But so is the nagging reality that we haven't arrived yet and something is wrong in our world. Humans are on a quest for an authentic reality that fulfills this universal desire.

Although the characters in this story are fictitious, the inner craving for reality expressed by Steve is not. And once we move past the surface questions like "Why can't people just get along?" we find ourselves asking deeper questions. "Where did we come from? Why do I exist? Is there really meaning and purpose in life?" These questions are also universal.

As a young man I wrestled with these same questions. Yet I eventually came to trust in a loving God who has purposefully created a complex and beautiful universe. But that doesn't mean this path to faith has been easy.

As I searched for a logical answer to the question

of origin, I found evolution to be insufficient. If evolution is powerful enough to convert pond scum into the incredible complexity of life we observe around us, it should also be able to resolve lesser issues like cancer and human relationships. If it is powerful enough to create our intricate ecosystem, why, after millions of years, can't people get along? This is a simple issue compared to evolving from an amoeba into something as complex as the human body. And further, evolution never even attempts to answer the larger question of where the original pond came from. Who put it there? People talk about the Big Bang, but they can't seem to explain what it was that banged or where those initial ingredients came from. If there is an effect, there must first be a cause. I cannot escape seeing evidence for a designer.

There is, however, a huge gap between believing in intelligent design to believing in the God of the Bible. As a young man, I was troubled when individuals tried to assert that the Bible is true solely because it says so. In an honest search for truth, one cannot assume the Bible is true by only using statements from the Bible to support that claim. This is poor logic, circular reasoning, and fails to answer the question of whether the Bible is trustworthy. But if we begin to investigate the historic underpinnings of the Bible, we find proofs that are not easily dismissed.

Frank Morison, a British journalist, thought he would do the world a great favor by disproving Christianity. He knew that the entire religion hangs on the authenticity of the resurrection, so that is where he started. But as he carefully examined the historical evidence and eyewitness accounts, he came to believe in it. He discovered that a close examination can be dangerous and can impact your life. He went on to write a defense of Christianity called *Who Moved the Stone?*[9]

Simon Greenleaf was an agnostic who believed that the resurrection of Jesus Christ was either a hoax or a myth. Greenleaf was a principle founder of Harvard Law School and an expert on evidence. When challenged by one of his students to consider the evidence for the resurrection of Jesus Christ, Greenleaf took up the challenge and set out to disprove it. But at the end of his investigation, he determined that the resurrection was indeed fact. He went on to say about the Bible:

Of the Divine character of the Bible, I

think, no man who deals honestly with his own mind and heart can entertain a reasonable doubt. For myself, I must say, that having for many years made the evidences of Christianity the subject of close study, the result has been a firm and increasing conviction of the authenticity and plenary inspiration of the Bible. It is indeed the Word of God.[10]

Lee Strobel was an investigative journalist for the *Chicago Tribune*. Strobel was a confident atheist until his wife converted to Christianity. Following this unnerving event, he decided to investigate the claims of Jesus Christ, specifically the account of the resurrection. Using the journalistic skills he had learned working for the *Tribune*, he went on an intensive investigative mission. The result was his conversion to Christianity. He authored a book titled *The Case for Christ*,[11] which documented his findings.

These are just a few of the men who went out to disprove the resurrection of Jesus Christ and came back changed men.

Beyond the historical record is the impact of seeing the teachings of Jesus put into practice. As I consider my own path to faith, I realize I have come to believe in absolute truth primarily by what I have witnessed. Christianity for me is not some abstract belief based solely on an in-depth study on Biblical authenticity, it is also based on observation.

All my life I have been surrounded by people who professed to be followers of Jesus Christ—people who helped each other in a crisis, cared for the weak, and looked for ways to bless each other. They were not perfect people. They made mistakes. They sometimes hurt other people's feelings, and at times got their own feelings hurt. Yet they persistently pursued a path of restoration.

They were people who really wanted to be like Jesus Christ, and His power was slowly changing them into His image. They saw the teachings of Jesus not as hard sayings, but as God's original intent for our world. God wants us to be loving and kind to each other. He desires a world where people are concerned about the hurting, and His church today is to be a demonstration of His desires for the world.

Though I have chosen to believe in and follow God, I want to be clear: I still have questions. There are things I don't understand.

I don't understand why God has allowed men to use the cross of Christ as a symbol for ungodly and hateful events like the Crusades. Jesus was very clear that his followers would not kill, and I don't understand why He allows people to claim they are following Him while promoting violence and military aggression. How can people claim to follow Jesus without following Him? Nor do I understand why certain countries continue to be bombarded with natural disasters and starvation, while other countries pay their farmers to reduce their agricultural production.

But neither do I comprehend why God created a world so resplendent with natural beauty and incredible diversity. Was it really necessary to use that many shades of color in a peacock? Do there really need to be over 300,000 different kinds of plants and 350,000 different species of beetles? And why are there so many different kinds of food to enjoy?

A Christian believes that God is good, so he naturally wrestles with human suffering. Although he has confidence that God will eventually work things out for good, there are times he will struggle with basic faith.

But an atheist also has things to wrestle with. What about pleasure, happiness, and beauty? Where did love and sympathy for the weak come from? These are obviously not required for natural selection— quite the opposite—so why do they exist? Why do we see such stunning sunsets on the evening horizon? And why that feeling of joy while watching a child laugh and play? Something deep within tells us this is more than just chance.

I see the goodness of God all around me. Although there are things I don't understand, I have observed enough of His goodness to trust Him for what I cannot yet understand. Some situations still seem wrong, but I live in confidence that a day is coming when all these wrongs will be made right.

I am convinced the problem isn't a shortage of verifiable facts regarding the existence of God. There is no lack of proof that a designer was needed to create the complexity and beauty that surrounds us.

While Jesus was on trial, Pilate, the Roman judge overseeing the proceedings, became perplexed. He had a Jewish mob crying out for crucifixion, yet he couldn't find any crime Jesus had committed. Finally, in exasperation, he turned to Jesus and asked a profound question: "What is truth?"[12] Pilate asked this extremely important question to the one person who had the answer. But ironically, he didn't wait for an answer. The Bible says he just walked away before Jesus could answer.

Many people today are asking the same question. They are verbalizing one of the most important questions a person can ask. And though answers are available, they are not taking time to investigate the facts. However, if you really want the truth, it is available. There are answers.

But the first question is this: "Are you willing to honestly investigate the evidence?"

If you have questions or would like to locate other followers of Jesus who are serious about doing what He says, please contact kingdomquestions@gmail.com.

Endnotes

[1] Job 14:14

[2] Job 21:15

[3] *The First Apology of Justin Martyr* (155-157 A.D. is a defense of the Christians who were being persecuted under the Roman Emperor. Justin was a philosopher who became convinced of the claims of Christianity. His writing is available online at: http://www.earlychristianwritings.com/text/justinmartyr-firstapology.html.

[4] The writings of Josephus reference Jesus two different times.

[5] *What's Wrong with the World*, G.K. Chesterton, 1910, Part 1, Chapter 5.

[6] John 14:6

[7] Mark 14:60-64; John 1:1-4; John 10:30

[8] *Mere Christianity*, C.S. Lewis, The MacMillan Company, 1960, p. 40.

[9] Frank Morison, *Who Moved The Stone?*, Zondervan Publishing, Grand Rapids, MI, 1958.

[10] *A Cloud of Witnesses,* Stephen Abbott Northrop, D.D., (Portland, Oregon: American Heritage Ministries, 1987), p. 198.

[11] Lee Strobel, *The Case for Christ,* Zondervan Publishing, Grand Rapids, MI, 1998.

[12] John 18:38

Additional Resources

I f you would like to learn more about the kingdom of God, the early Christians, or Christian apologetics, here are some additional resources you may want to consider:

More Than a Carpenter
Josh McDowell
This small book focuses on the question of who Jesus really was. It addresses what was so unique about Jesus and why it is intellectually inconsistent to only call Him a "Good Teacher." He was either the Lord, a liar, or a lunatic!

The Case for Christ

Lee Strobel

This book is written by a skeptic who decided to investigate the Christian religion. The book chronicles his investigation. It is a good book for the intellectual, the doubter, and the inquisitive skeptic who sincerely wants to discover the truth.

Who Moved The Stone?

Frank Morison

Written almost as a confession, this book was authored by a man whose purpose was to expose the Christian religion as fraudulent. He set out to prove that the resurrection never occurred. His investigation uncovered so many irrefutable historical facts that he ultimately came to faith in Jesus Christ.

The Kingdom That Turned the World Upside Down

David Bercot

This is an excellent work on the early Christians. It describes their love for the kingdom of God and the impact their devotion to Jesus made on the Roman world. If you are serious about seeking God and learning about the early church, this is a good resource.

Other Books by Gary Miller

The author has written over twenty books on various topics and for different audiences. For a complete listing of his resources and a description of each one, visit TGS International's website at tgsinternational.com.

Kingdom-Focused Living Series

Kingdom-Focused Finances for the Family
Charting a Course in Your Youth
Going Till You're Gone
It's Not Your Business
The Other Side of the Wall

Manuals for Developing Countries

    A Good Soldier of Jesus Christ

    Following Jesus in Everyday Life

Full-Color Graph Books

    Life in a Global Village

    This Side of the Global Wall

Technology

    Surviving the Tech Tsunami

    Tech Talk

Other

    Jesus and Proverbs

    Reaching America

    Jesus Really Said That?

    How Can Anyone Say God Is Good?

    Church Matters

About the Author

Gary Miller was raised in California and today lives with his wife Patty and family in the Pacific Northwest. Gary works with the poor in developing countries and directs the SALT Microfinance Solutions program for Christian Aid Ministries. This program offers business and spiritual teaching to those living in chronic poverty, provides small loans, sets up local village savings groups, and assists them in learning how to use their God-given resources to become sustainable.

Gary has authored the Kingdom-Focused Living series, microfinance manuals, and several booklets for outreach purposes.

Have you been inspired by Gary's materials? Maybe you have questions, or perhaps you even disagree with the author. Share your thoughts by sending an email to kingdomfinance@camoh.org.